Text © 1990 Susan Hill
Illustrations © 1990 Jim Bispham
All rights reserved
First published in Great Britain 1990 by
Julia MacRae Books
A division of Walker Books Ltd
87 Vauxhall Walk London SE11 5HJ

Printed and bound in Hong Kong by
South China Printing Co. (1988) Ltd.

Hill, Susan, 1942 -
I won't go there again
I. Title II. Bispham, Jim
823'.914 [J]

ISBN 0-86203-429-9

I WON'T GO THERE AGAIN

Susan Hill

With pictures by Jim Bispham

Julia MacRae Books

A DIVISION OF WALKER BOOKS

On Monday, Ben went to nursery school.
He stayed until twelve o'clock when his
mother came to collect him.

"Did you play with the sand and water?"
she asked.

"Yes," said Ben, "but I didn't like Lawrence.
He pushed. I won't go there again."
"Just keep out of his way," said his mother.

On Tuesday, after school, they went to the park.
"Did you have fun on the slide this morning?"
asked Ben's mother.

"Yes," said Ben, "but I didn't like Emma. She stuck out her tongue. I won't go there again."
"Don't look at her then," said his mother.

On Wednesday, Ben's grandmother came to lunch.

"Did you enjoy your milk and biscuits at school?"
she asked him.

"Yes," said Ben, "but I didn't like Michael.
He snatched. I won't go there again."
"Play with somebody else tomorrow,"
his grandmother said.

On Thursday, Ben and his mother got on
a bus and went to town.
"Did you play with all the toy cars at
school?" Ben's mother asked him.
"Yes," said Ben, "but I didn't like Lucy.
She screamed and screamed. I won't go
there again."

"Put your hands over your ears another day," said his mother.

On Friday, Ben's father collected
him from school.
"Had a good morning?"
he asked Ben.

"Yes," said Ben, "but I didn't like Neil. He trod on my toe. I won't go there again."
"I shouldn't think he did it on purpose," said his father.

On Saturday, there was no nursery school.

Ben's mother was busy decorating the bathroom.
Ben's father was busy working on the car.

Ben didn't have much to do.

On Sunday, they were going to the country for a picnic. But when they got up it was raining. "Never mind," said Ben's mother, "school again tomorrow."

That week at the nursery,
Sarah snatched,

Katie pinched,

James wouldn't share,

Duncan splashed
red paint,

and Roland and Mark kept on fighting.

"I didn't like anybody," said Ben to his
mother. "I won't go there again."

Later, they went to cousin Tony's house.
Ben and Tony climbed the big fir tree in the
garden. But Ben fell off and hurt his arm.

At the hospital, a doctor with a beard took a photograph of it. "Hm," he said, "we'll have to put that in plaster."

"No school for you tomorrow," said a smiley nurse.

All next day at home, Ben was fed up and his arm hurt. His mother read him stories and he watched children's television, but after that there wasn't anything much for him to do. At tea-time, Ben's nursery school teacher came to see him. She brought Ben a very big card, with GET WELL SOON BEN on the front.

"Inside are the names of all your friends," she said. Then she gave Ben a lot of sheets of paper. "Everybody's painted a picture for you to cheer you up. You can pin them on the bedroom wall."

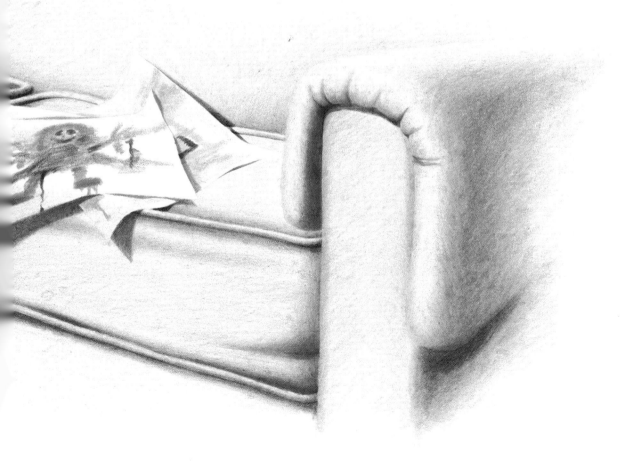

The next morning after breakfast, Ben got his coat. "I'm going to school," he said.

"You won't be able to do much because of your arm," his mother told him.

"I know," said Ben, "I just want to be with all my friends."

That week at school Ben had a wonderful time.

James drew a caterpillar on his
plaster. Sarah gave him half her biscuit.
Katie sat next to him at story-time.
Duncan told him an elephant joke.

Mark lent him his new space-rocket.
And Lucy invited him to her party.

"Well," asked Ben's mother on Friday,
"how were things at school?"
"Good," said Ben, "I liked everybody."

On Saturday, Ben and his father went on to the Common to fly Ben's kite. Lawrence and his dad were there, too.

"Hello there, Lawrence," said Ben's father. "How are you getting on at school?"

"All right," said Lawrence, "but I don't like Ben. He put a worm in my boots. I won't go there again."

"That's what I used to say," said Ben.